PANNING GOLD

WHAT
THE BEGINNER
NEEDS TO KNOW

WRITTEN ESPECIALLY
FOR
BEGINNER PROSPECTORS

BY

THE OLD PROSPECTOR

WRITTEN
FROM
EXPERIENCE

INTRODUCTION

Gold Mining is divided into two distinct classes, Lode Mining and Placer Mining. This booklet only deals with Placer Mining on a small scale, but for your information we will describe Lode Mining so you will know where the difference is.

There is not too much known about how gold was made but we do know that all gold was originally "lode gold." Lode gold is that which is in the ore of different kinds and placer gold is that which has been freed from the ore by some action of Nature such as erosion. Lode Mining is freeing the gold from the ore and recovering it. Placer Mining is recovering the free gold or other minerals from the gravel, sand, clay or dirt where Nature deposited it through water action.

Beginner Prospectors at first are more interested in where they can go to do their Gold Panning and Placer Mining. Most of the known placer fields in North America are in the western part. There is a wide belt extending from the islands in Bering Sea in the Arctic Circle, down through Alaska, Western Canada, the United States and down into Mexico. This belt runs from the Pacific Ocean in some places to the foothills on the eastern slope of the Rocky Mountains. In this belt are the western placer fields. There are other scattered placer fields one of the largest being in the Black Hills of the Dakotas and another large belt runs through North Carolina down through into Georgia. There are many other small ones that are known and no doubt there are many placer fields in the U. S. buried so deep they have not been found.

SOME GOOD ADVICE
From
THE OLD PROSPECTOR

No doubt there is a lot of information in this booklet that the experienced prospector could be benefited by. Fundamentally though, it has been written for the beginner, the one who does not know what a gold pan or sluice box or even gold looks like.

This book is not going to tell you all about placering, only the things that a beginner needs to know as the title states. It is more to get you started off on the right foot and not spend too much time or money in finding out by experience how to go about making a prospector out of yourself.

It is true that not more than half of the men that took up placer mining during the Gold Rush days made much more than a living by placering. It wasn't because the gold wasn't there to be found, but mostly because they did not know how to go about recovering it. At that time they were finding gold close to the surface and sometimes on the surface of the bedrock in the rivers and arroyos.

It is a different story today, not that there isn't gold to be found, for there is. There is many more times as much gold in the ground than has been taken out. But it does not lay in plain sight like in the old days. Now we have to go below the surface and find it. This is not too hard, for Nature left sign boards of different kinds telling us where she hid those yellow bits of metal.

How to read those signboards, how to figure the line of travel the gold took as it was washed down the rivers and creeks, and to tell from the surface indications where more or less of the gold was deposited is why the prospector that does know gets so much more gold than the man that does not know.

If you have a trade, you know how much work an outsider that does not know your trade would do on your job until he had learned something about it. And so it is with placering. If you don't know something about it, you don't get any gold.

But you are not in the position that the "gold rush" prospectors were. They couldn't get books to read to tell them how to do it. They couldn't get the kind of tools and the modern equipment that we have today. They had to work with crude equipment and guess about where the gold was and learn how to recover it through experience and that was a slow, tedious job.

But now there are hundreds of books written on modern methods of mining, and you can obtain blue-prints that show you how to build modern machines for recovering gold. All of those things that those old timers would have been glad to have are yours at very little cost.

Even though there was more gold and it was closer to the surface in the old days, the placer miner of today has many things in his favor. The experienced prospect-or knows pretty close to where the gold is concentrated. He can handle twenty times as much gravel with his modern equipment as the old timer could and make 25 to 40% better recovery.

But if you don't know how to do it or what kind of equipment to use you are not as well off as the "gold rush-er" for he did not have to look underneath for his gold like you have to do today. That's a long way of saying you better learn about placer mining before you start out with the intentions of having the gold you get pay your expenses and also wages.

DIFFERENT KINDS OF PLACER MINING

Placer mining is divided into different classes. Dredging, which is also divided into different classes—Drag Line, Bucket and Suction Dredging. Drag Line dredging is where the gravel is scooped up with a bucket and dumped into a floating boat that contains equipment for recovering the gold. Bucket Line dredging is where a continuous line of buckets brings up the gravel and dump it into recovering equipment. Suction dredging is where the gravel is sucked up by a pump, usually a centrifugal pump, and run through recovery equipment.

Hydraulic placer mining is where the gold bearing gravel is washed off the sides of the hills by a powerful stream of water and the gold is caught by riffles in sluice boxes that the gravel runs through.

Ground sluicing is the same as hydraulic placer mining except on a small scale.

Now we come to the pick and shovel placering which most of you are concerned with at the present. This, we will have to divide into two classes: Wet and dry placering.

Wet placering is using water to separate the gold from the aggregate and dry placering is using air forcing the lighter material away from the gold by bellows or fan action.

The gold pan came first and has been used in some form for recovering gold for ages. They come in different  sizes and shapes, from the 6" clean up to the 20" batea type pan. The batea type pan is only about 1¾" deep with a bottom two inches across. It has a heavy curled rim around the edge for catching the gold and a hole in the rim to get the gold out. They are not practical except for cleaning up concentrates as it is easy to separate the gold from the black sand in the small bottom.

Some pans have ridges on the sides of the pan called riffles which extend about one-fourth of the distance around the pan. They are called riffle pans. They do help the beginner a little in saving the gold but it is best not to use them as eventually you will want to use the standard steel pan for quicker work. Farther on in the book you will find a complete panning lesson.

The pick and shovel man uses different kinds of equipment for recovering the gold with water. The Papoose (rocking sluice), the dip box which is a stationary box that water is dipped into is too slow, the rocking sluice is so much better you will not want to use it. The Doodle Bug, a wet concentrator using a gas engine, pump and hose and the Sluice Box.

The Papoose is pictured below.

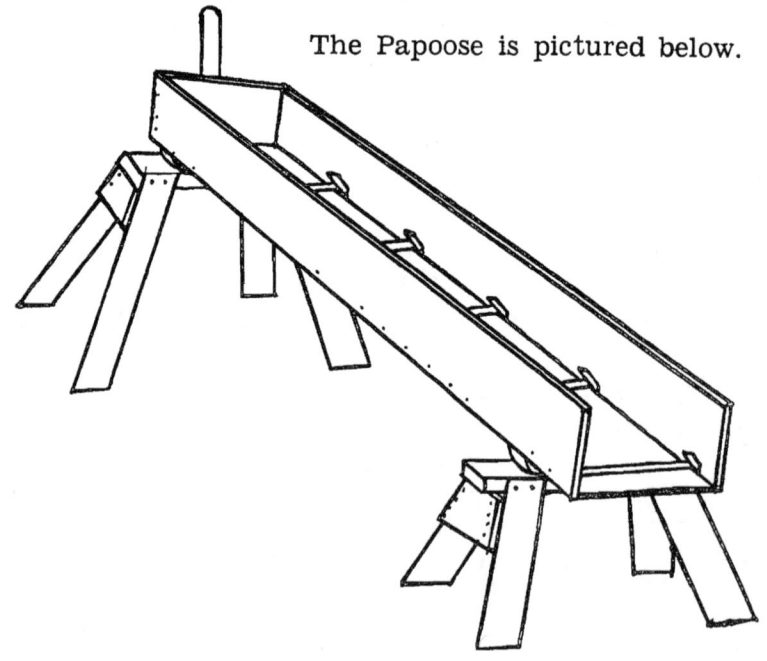

When using the Papoose the prospector puts one or two shovels of gravel in the box, then dips water into the box and starts rocking at the same time. It does not require much water and if water is scarce it can be used over and over. It will recover 95% of the gold when the gravel is dry and more than that when shoveling gravel out of water. It can be made light and easily carried to hard to get to places. The small machines only weigh about twenty-five pounds.

The Doodle Bug is pictured below.

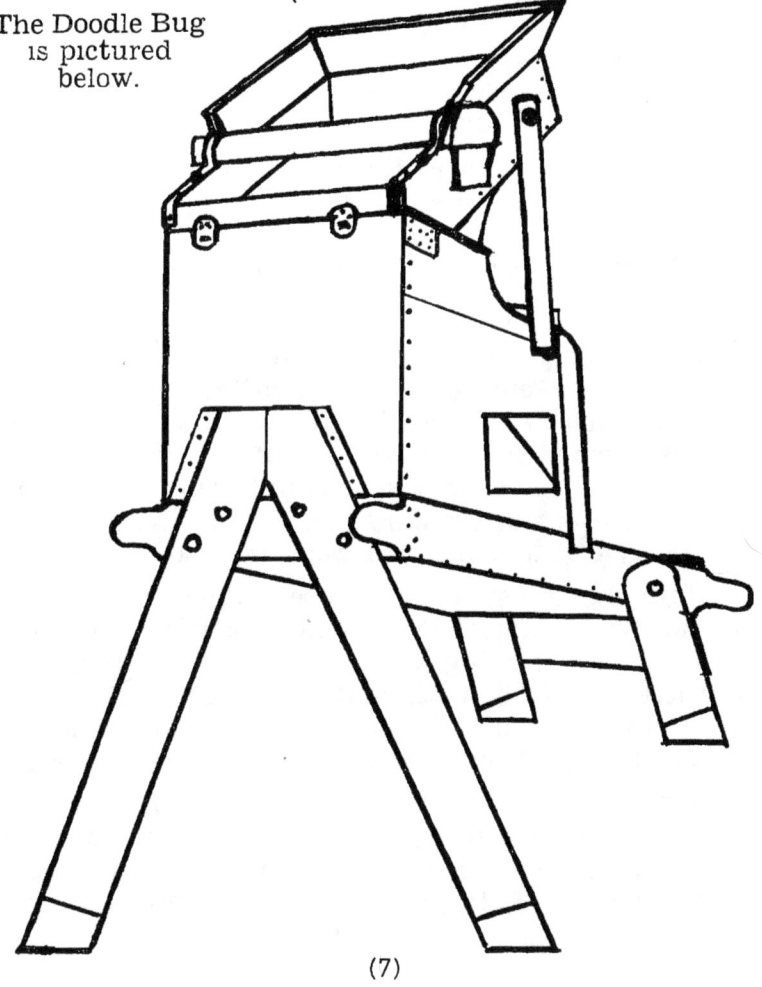

Nearly all wet placer machines have to be set up close to a water supply. The Doodle Bug is set up where the pay dirt is and the gas engine and pump is placed near the water supply. Your range to work in is only limited by the amount of hose you have.

The hose is connected to the pipe shown above the hopper and sprays the gravel that is shoveled into the hopper, the wet gravel slides down the hopper, reverses direction and slides over a trommel made of ¼" rods, the fines drop through the trommel and the rocks drop out the sides of the box. When the fines drop through the grid they hit a return pan that carries them to the front of the screen box.

A puddling movement takes place in the head of the screen box which makes the Doodle Bug such a good recovery machine. It is quick to clean up, weighs only about 40 pounds, can be dismantled quickly and packed in car.

A 5/8 horsepower gas engine and a ¾" outlet pump will pump water enough for the Doodle Bug. If gravel is being shoveled out of water, the machine will take all the gravel two men can shovel and if the ground has to be picked, two men cannot keep it full even if the ground is dry. Recovery in ordinary river bar gravel is around 95% in dry dirt and more in wet aggregate.

Sluice boxes can only be used when water conditions are right and that does not happen very often. But if you are placering where the water is swift enough and there is enough water and the ground you wish to work lies where you can ditch the water to it and can run the tailings back into the river, then, the sluice box is the best equipment to use.

Sluice boxes are used in strings, the upper boxes are used to bring the water without losing elevation, then a box to shovel into, to give the gold a chance to drop down before it reaches the screen box which is set just below the shovel-in box, below that are the tailing boxes which carry the tailings to the river.

The grade on the head boxes is just so the water will flow good, the shovel-in box is set steep enough so the water will move the gravel from one shovel, before the next shovel full is put in; the screen box is set just steep enough so that the aggregate keeps moving and the tail boxes are set the same way.

How to set up and work sluice boxes is explained in the book, Gold In Placer, also in the Panning Gold booklets listed in catalog, also the advantages of using different kinds of screens and riffles. The blueprint on sluice boxes shows different methods of making them and joining them together.

The Long Tom is something similar to the Papoose only larger, costs more to build, is much heavier and uses more water, so instead we use the Papoose, which is lighter, handles more dirt, and gets more gold.

The Rocker, still used by many prospectors, is another obsolete machine as far as the man who has to get some gold or he doesn't eat, is concerned.

The Cradle, too, is clumsy and heavy for ordinary gravel, although there are times when there is so much clay in the gravel that a machine like this has to be used. You probably will never run across that kind of aggregate so we will not describe it here.

That covers about all the wet placer machines that are used today. In the book, Gold In Placer, how to work all of these machines is explained fully. In the chapter, The Man Who Knows How, you are taken on a two weeks trip, placering with a Doodle Bug. The author explains all about everything you do on that trip, and why you do it.

It is explained to you in such a way you will know all about what he has done, right from the time you reach the placer ground until the gold is ready to sell to the buyer. He does not leave anything to your imagination.

DRY PLACER MACHINES

When water is not available and the sand or gravel is thoroughly dry, gold is recovered with dry washers. Most dry washers are of the bellows type. Some of them using vibration and some of them using a fan.

The bellows machine is the most popular one in the portable machines. They weigh from 8 pounds (The Sampler) to power dry washers that weigh 300 pounds.

The smallest is the Sampler, a bellows type machine that folds up and can be carried under the arm. It is used mostly for tracing leads but can also be used for testing placer deposits.

The next is the hand machine which, in the modern type, weighs about 32 pounds. Some of the old time hand dry washers weighed as much as 200 pounds. There is also the power dry washer, which gets its power from a small gasoline engine. The modern type weighs about fifty pounds with gas engine. It is also a bellows type machine and in addition has a vibrating screen. The bellows blast about 150 times a minute and the screen vibrates around 900 times a minute. The engine is a two cycle aluminum gas engine that weighs only 17 pounds. It will keep one man busy with loose dirt.

It must be remembered though, that none of these air machines are efficient if the dirt is not dry. They will not save gold at all if there is 40% of moisture present. Where they could save 98% if the dirt was perfectly dry, the percentage of recovery will drop three times as fast as the percentage of moisture increases.

THE HAND DRY WASHER

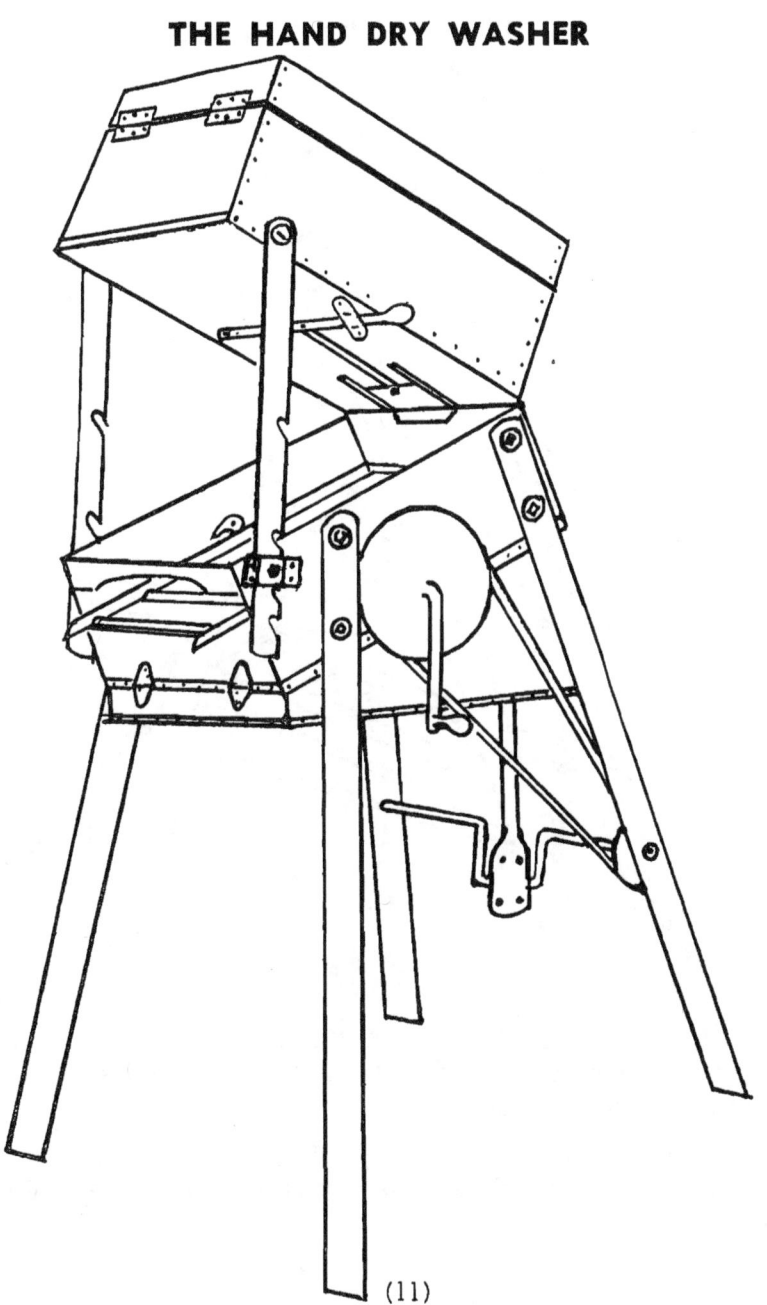

THE POWER DRY WASHER

Recovering gold by the dry method is not as fast as using water and the value per yard must be considerably more to make it profitable.

There is one more way of recovering gold that should be mentioned as sooner or later you will be using it.

When gold particles are so small that they cannot be separated by ordinary panning, it is necessary to use the amalgamation process. This is done by bringing the fine particles in contact with quicksilver. The quicksilver will quickly envelope the gold and then as the quicksilver can easily be brought back together and can be quickly separated from other foreign material. The quicksilver is then separated from the gold as much as possible by passing it through a tight weave cloth which will let the quicksilver pass through but hold the gold. It is then called amalgam. Retorting then separates the gold from the quicksilver.

One other item that is used in dry placering is the bib, it can be used to quickly concentrate the gold and black sand. It is a frame made of 1"x1" pieces about 8"x14" with canvas tacked on the bottom. It is handled a lot like a gold pan is.

A blueprint showing how to build a combination grub box and table, a retort and a bib is listed in the back of this book.

Blueprints are also listed covering the Papoose, Doodle Bug, sluice boxes and the Sampler, Hand and Power Dry Washers.

Blueprinted maps are also listed showing known placer districts in all the western states, also maps covering the lode districts where lode gold has been found.

If you are interested in Lode Prospecting, you will find a description of the book, Gold In Lode, which all Prospectors should read.

The blueprints of the machines listed in the back are drawn so that the average man can read them. Details are shown and lettered which makes it easy for you to locate on the large drawings where that part goes, most of the blueprints also have an instruction sheet giving you suggestions that will make the building of them easier.

THE ART OF PANNING GOLD

Here is a few "don'ts" to start off with in telling you how to swish a gold pan with good results.

Don't use a greasy pan, new pans are greased to keep them from rusting, be sure yours is clean, rub it good with sand and water. Don't pan in swift water or where the water is choppy. Don't try to pan in a position where you are balancing yourself.

Spend some time making a good panning hole, it should be twice as deep as the depth of your pan and twice the width of your pan. Make it in a place where the water will flow through it, keeping the water clean. Dirty water is hard to pan in. Sit down on a large rock and put one leg on each side of the panning hole. The more comfortable you are the better you will be able to control the water.

Fill your pan level full of gravel. With the pan under water, mix the gravel with your hands, making little holes between the gravel for the gold to drop through. Most of your work in panning is trying to make places for the gold to drop through. After you have it mixed up good and with the pan still under water, grasp the pan with your hands exactly opposite. Give the pan a good shaking, still under water, with a half circle movement and a to and from you movement. Now bring the pan to the top of the water and let the water drain off at a point opposite you. Notice that when it drains off it takes some of the lighter dirt with it.

Moving the light dirt out of the pan with water is called sloughing. How fast you can move that lighter material out of the pan and not let any gold go with it determines how fast a panner you are. One good rule is to always move some dirt out of the pan every time you run water out. Here is one little trick that saves a lot of time. When you make your last few shakes, tilt the pan away from you so that when you are through shaking the dirt will be close to the lip of the pan. Then when you make your dip hold the pan at that same tilt and when the water runs off, it will not have as far to carry the dirt.

Always dip your pan so that the water will come to the back edge of the pan until your pan is nearly empty. You will find that most of the lighter material is of a lighter color and the heavier material of a darker color.

As the larger rocks show up and are washed off clean, throw them out. Always keep your pan under water when you are scratching the larger rocks out. Don't shake the pan out of water, always under water.

Panning is a continuation of sloughing and shaking, usually five or six shakes of the pan is enough and the same number of dips. If you shake too much you are losing time and if you dip too many times you are losing gold. After each shake you will notice the material on top is of a lighter color and after you have made a few dips it will get darker, use this color to go by to know when you have dipped enough and it is time to shake again.

When you dip, do not shove the pan away from you under the water, push it straight down and when the water has covered the material, raise it straight up, keeping the pan tilted at the same angle as you had it when you quit shaking and had the dirt at the lip of the pan.

After you have nothing left in the pan apparently but black sand you must be more careful with your dipping and do more shaking to the number of dips. You are now working with heavier material and it is harder for the gold to drop through this heavy stuff.

When you become more proficient you can keep dipping and sloughing until the colors that are on the surface are close to the lip of the pan before shaking again.

After you have the amount of black sand down to where you can cover it with your thumb, place your left hand to the left side of the pan and the right hand at the center away from you so that your thumb can reach the bottom of the pan. Work the black sand into a small pile below your right hand. Place your thumb over the black sand and gold, (if there is any gold), and dip about a cup of water into the pan.

Tilt the pan so the water is under your left hand, then tip it slowly so the water will run by your thumb a couple inches, then tip the other way and the water will run by you thumb and over and around the black sand. Notice that a few grains of black sand will go with the water. Continue this movement, gradually turning the pan and working your hands to the right on the pan to keep away from the black sand that is accumulating to the left. If you do not have all the black sand out of the gold by the time you are around the pan, hold your thumb over what concentrates are left and wash all the excess black sand out of the pan. Then continue the same movements until all of the black sand has been taken from the gold.

Sure—you can throw some quicksilver in the pan and pick up that fine gold in a few minutes, but here is the catch. After gold has been amalgamated or refined in any way, shape or manner, you must sell it to the Government at $35 an ounce—1,000 fine and as the average placer gold does not run better than 925 fine, you will not get much over $31 an ounce. But, at present you can get $35 to $40 an ounce "as is," regardless of fineness which will make a difference of more than 50c a pennyweight for the gold you get.

(16)

After you have taken out all the gold you can by panning, there will still be some small particles left. Some of them you will not be able to see with the naked eye. Then you can use the quicksilver and pick up what it left. The quicksilver will pick it up regardless of how small it is.

Sometimes when you are using quicksilver in recovery, the quicksilver will roll right over a piece of gold and sometimes over a lot of the gold in the pan. It means that there is some kind of a foreign matter on the gold, such as a greasy substance that comes off of clay, or it may be rusted on account of small particles of iron sticking to it. Then your concentrates must be scrubbed. Use a flat rock and run this through your concentrates, this will clean the gold of foreign material.

If you have some gold with matrix attached to it, (usually a white quartz) don't try to pick it up with the quicksilver. That foreign substance will eventually be burned out before your gold is sold. That also applies to any foreign substance in your amalgam.

Even after you have burned your amalgam to where you think it is perfectly clean, when you take it to the gold buyer he will burn it again with a torch and will take an average of one grain out of each pennyweight.

If you are one of those prospectors who are depending on your day's take to pay for your beans and buns, don't waste your time cleaning up your concentrates through the day. Wait until the end of the day and clean all that you have accumulated at one time. Some of our best prospectors only do this once a week as they save a lot of time.

Only practice will make you perfect in panning gold. Every panner has his own movements for getting the gold to the bottom of the pan and you will have yours. The most important thing is to have confidence in yourself in controlling the water.

SOME GOOD ADVICE TO THE BEGINNER

Anything worth doing at all is worth doing well. Whether your placer mining is to be just a hobby or to supplement a small pension, income, or a full time job, learn to do it right and you will get more pleasure and profit from it.

There is nothing more discouraging than to go on a panning trip and come home without even a color to show, or to spend that long looked for vacation on a placering trip and when it's time to go home, only have enough gold to cover the bottom of a small bottle.

In my thirty years of placering off and on, I've seen hundreds, yes—probably thousands of beginners that never graduated from the beginner class, and never recovered enough gold to pay for their tobacco much less their beans and buns or expenses. Probably 25% of them failed on account of lack of energy, or did not find a string of colors in a pan to get them interested enough, but the balance failed BECAUSE THEY DIDNT KNOW HOW.

As the book, Gold In Placer, says, "There's millions of tons of dirt in a placer field, but if you don't move the right ton you DON'T get the gold." Placer mining can be learned by experience, but it takes a long time and a lot of hard work. It takes experience to become a good panner, but you can quickly learn to pan by experience after you have read how to do it. And it's the same with the rest of the art of finding and recovering those yellow particles that Nature did such a good job hiding.

Nature did leave signboards, telling us where she hid that gold and knowing how to read those signboards will most likely spell the difference between coming home with a few colors or a bottle you will be proud to show.

(18)

THE BEGINNER'S DILEMMA

You are on a placering trip. Pick, shovel, pan, camping equipment, lots of grub and energy. You arrive at a gold bearing river, pitch your camp and just what are you going to do next?

That river bar down below you is just a big bunch of rocks and sand. Anyway you are going to try out that new pan. So you go down to the river, find some gravel that is easy to shovel, fill your pan and go through some motions that resemble panning. Results, no gold, not even a color, and it's supposed to be a gold bearing river. You try another pan, same results.

What did you do wrong? It's a good bet that you were panning some gravel that was washed in after the pay streaks were made and it's seldom that you get any gold from gravel that is on the surface and easy to shovel.

The river bar might look like a bunch of rocks and sand to you, but to the man "who knows how," it doesn't. He can stand in one place and point out to you, the places on that bar, where you are most liable to find the concentration points, pockets or pay streaks.

It's too late now, you should have learned something before you started out. You will go on panning. You might be lucky and stumble on to a pocket that had so much gold that you couldn't help but recover some of it in your pan, but it is a pretty safe bet that you will get discouraged and disgusted before the first day is over.

How different would have been the results of your trip as far as the amount of gold you recovered was concerned or the satisfaction you received from the trip if you had read the book, Gold In Placer.

There wouldn't have been enough hours in the day to give you time to pan all the places that looked promising to you from what you had learned.

So—use your "noggin." Learn something about where to look for those concentration points before spending a lot of money on equipment you will not use or ruining that precious vacation running around the country looking for placer grounds. You can save enough money in one day on your gas bill to pay for all your books and maps that will give you the information you should have.

Knowing just a little about placer mining makes a tremendous difference in how much gold you will recover and it doesn't take long to learn that little by reading a good book on the subject like, Gold In Placer.

The Bureau of Mines of California gives us some interesting data about what happened during the last depression to all of those beginner prospectors that flocked to the gold bearing streams of California to scratch out a meager living in preference to being on the dole.

During the depression there were thousands of them along the rivers and it is easy to see that the Bureau of Mines was close to the right figures when they state that the average amount made by these people was between 30 and 50c per day.

Not a very pretty picture for the beginner that is starting out today. After you have learned something about placering though, you can easily see why their take was that small. I know personally that those figures are not far off as I spent most of the depression in the placer fields, and what I learned as that time was what prompted me to write the book, Gold In Placer. If that depression, looming on the horizon at present, keeps coming, the information in that book will make a lot of difference in the amount the readers will be able to recover.

WHERE TO LOOK FOR PLACER GOLD

All placer gold is deposited by water action, whether it is in the rivers, river bars, or old dry river channels on top of the hills. And you want to keep that fact in your mind continually when you are out there on that dry desert. Figuring where to look for it, you must picture in your mind how the water was running when it was deposited. And don't let that growth of vegetation or trees disrupt your picture, they may have grown there in the past hundred years but the gold may have been deposited thousands of years ago.

The small particles of gold that have been freed from the quartz veins are gradually washing down the hills until they come to some kind of a gully or creek, and if they do not concentrate at some obstruction, are carried down to the rivers and out into the ocean.

It is safe to say that 95% of the gold that is deposited in the rivers, creeks, or river bars is caused by a whip in the water that was caused by some kind of a natural riffle. If the water keeps moving fast it will keep carrying the gold along with it, but as it passes these natural obstructions an eddy of a certain degree is formed. This causes a centrifugal movement and that movement will tend to whip the heavier particles to one side, or if the obstruction just slows the water it will cause a downward whip that will whip the gold downward and as the force of the water has been lessened it loses its grip on the gold and the gold is deposited and will stay there until a heavier flow of water comes along and removes the obstruction.

If you are a fisherman that fishes in the trout streams on the mountain slopes, you look for places where there are obstructions in the river to do your fishing. That is because those obstructions slow the water, the trout will stay around that slow water and watch for particles of food coming down the faster water and dart out and get it. Where those trout wait for their dinner is a very good place to look for gold if it is a gold bearing river.

Remember—Any place in the creek or river that obstructs the flow of water or diverts it in a different direction is a possible concentration point. Just where around that obstruction is the exact point to look is something else and is determined by the amount of water and how the water goes by the obstruction.

Always, below an obstruction, there is more or less of a hole or depression. If the water is coming straight over the obstruction and there is enough depression, the gold will be deposited where the water comes up out of the hole or if there is enough force to the water it will be where it starts to level off. Very seldom in the bottom of the hole. If the obstruction caused the water to whirl and it would if it went around the obstruction, then the gold would be deposited to one side or even below the swirl depending on how much force there was to the water. These instructions apply mostly where you are working a shallow stream and bed rock or false bedrock is close to the surface.

If you are working on river gravel bars, bed rock might be ten to fifty feet down, then you would be looking for pay streaks. Pay streaks in the river bars are formed during storms when a large amount of water comes down the river and are always formed where there is a bend in the river and on the inside of the arc that the bend makes.

How to work these river bars and locate the pay streaks is discussed thoroughly in the book, Gold In Placer.

We've told you where to look for the gold when you found the gold bearing river or the placer field. Where to look for those rivers that are gold bearing and where those placer fields are located was a question to the beginner prospector until the Old Prospector spent a couple of years making up maps of the western states, British Columbia and Alaska showing where the known placer grounds are. Also maps showing where gold has been found in lode. Those maps are listed in the back of this booklet.

There is no doubt but what there are many placer fields in the country that no one knows about that are covered with more or less overburden. The beginner wants to see some gold and to recover some of it now, he is not so much interested at first about finding new deposits.

A "bajada" is the accumulation of material that has washed down the sides of the mountain and spread out as an alluvial fan at the base. While this material was being washed down, the gold veins on the sides of the mountain were being eroded away and the gold was being freed from the ore. Account of the gold being heavier than the rest of the aggregate it kept dropping through the moving material and by the time the bottom of the mountain or hill is reached it is concentrated more or less and the balance of the material passes over it. This alluvial fan may extend for a mile away from the mountain, but down underneath there somewhere is a deposit of gold.

There's probably thousands of these bajadas in the desert country of the western part of the United States.

GOLD

What makes gold so fascinating? There are many things about gold in addition to its value as a medium of exchange.

I used to say that nothing else looks like gold. I had to change my mind on that, there is something else. We have a black sand in the river where I live, that when it is put under a violet light looks like it was fifty per cent gold. It has the actual gold color. But when you are working at placering there is nothing you will find that looks exactly like gold.

We have what we call "fool's gold" but it does not look exactly like gold, it only shines from one side and can be broken with the thumb nail. It does have a look something like gold when it is under water. It is scales from pyrite mostly.

Gold can be hammered so thin it would take fifty thicknesses of it to be as thick as the paper this is written on. I once found a piece of gold about two inches long and three-quarters of an inch wide that was so thin that you could read this print through it. Its value in money about 6c. Gold will not break when hit with a hammer but will flatten. There is only a couple of the elements that are heavier than gold.

Gold can be manufactured, but it costs more to manufacture it than the result would be worth. Gold from different placer fields has a slightly different color, from a lighter yellow to a deeper yellow. The cause of the lighter color is the foreign material in the gold. When you are placering and the gold is real light in that district where you are working, you will find you will not get as much for it from the gold buyer as you will the gold with a deeper yellow color.

SIDE LINES TO PANNING GOLD

The prospector of today does not wait to trip over a ledge and discover it is full of gold, or have his burro kick an out-cropping and find it is a rich lead.

We have the Mineralight that shows us what is inside of a rock and in some cases will tell what kind of mineral the rock contains; the M-Scope that will tell us about the magnetic ore that is buried in the ground, and the Geiger Counter that will locate uranium by picking up the emanations.

There are many sides to your placer mining that could prove profitable. When you are cleaning a piece of bedrock and run across a ledge that contains ore or a seam that cuts across the bedrock, it should be investigated, it could easily be the seam that the placer gold you have been getting came from.

And in your prospecting for placer ground, you do considerable roaming. You cross hills to get to another gulch and you should inform yourself, so you will be able to tell if those outcroppings and ledges would carry anything of value. Keep remembering that the placer gold came from gold ore seams and they may be right in the district where you are finding placer gold.

The book, Gold In Lode, written for the beginner prospector will give you a lot of this information. If you find a piece of float on the hillside, the book will tell you how to trace that piece of float to its source. A large percentage of the rich mines that have been found were located by tracing back to where the piece of float came from.

Learn the signboards for lode mining same as you do for placer mining, it may be the way you will find that stake that will put you on easy street for the rest of your life.

SOME DONT'S

In the mountainous regions it is usually hard to get to the river except where the roads cross them. Beginner prospectors have a habit of wanting to do their panning and placering close to these roads.

You must stop and think. Hundreds of prospectors have done the same thing and the result is that the ground along the river close to the highways or roads or bridges have been panned continuously and therefore have very little gold left in the bars and banks.

You must keep this in mind when you are choosing your equipment, you are not going to drive right to the spot where there are some good concentration points. There probably were some good concentration points there at one time but usually they are worked out. So you are going to pack your equipment farther away from the highway and the farther you go your pickings will be just that much better.

Some of our best placering ground left in California that has not been worked out, lies in a stretch of ground between the Feather River on the north to below the Yosemite Park on the south, not too high to be out of the gold district, but too far away from the highways for the average prospector to want to tackle it.

It is rough country and hard to get around in and because that is so is why it has not been worked out. You can go for miles in there and not see a sign of a human being or any signs of his having been there. It is in those kind of places that you find the virgin ground and good pickings, not around the highways that cross the rivers or the placer grounds that a good road leads to. Everything that is good is hard to get at and this also applies to placer mining.

CAMPING EQUIPMENT

Everyone has their own ideas about the kind of camping equipment they want. Here is a few ideas that may help you.

In sleeping equipment, an air mattress and a sleeping bag will give you more comfort per pound weight than anything else. A cot is nice but they are the coldest things imaginable and are quite heavy. A good sleeping bag on some branches and pine needles is pretty comfy.

If you are going to pack equipment, any kind of stove is taboo, a light wire grid that can be placed across your camp fire is quite a help. An aluminum skillet that has a handle that folds over. Of course you need some sharp knives, but for knives and forks, get those made of plastic, easy to clean and light to carry, also plastic cups and dishes.

The more comfortable your camp is and the more equipment you have makes for a more enjoyable trip but if one has to pack he will have to strike a happy medium in what he can take and what he can't take.

A single burner gas lantern and a gasoline stove are indispensible if you can drive to your camping ground. Also take along some kind of contraption to set in the river to keep your perishables in.

Don't forget to get a fire permit.

Your shovel should be a short handled, round point shovel, unless you are going to do some heavy placering then you will want a long handled shovel. A drift pick pointed at both ends with a double bitted axe handle in it is the lightest and best pick.

You should have a 16" gold pan for each one in the party and a 6 or 12" pan for accumulating concentrates.

Don't forget the snake bite kit, they are cheap insurance.

(27)

WET PLACERING VS. DRY PLACERING

I get hundreds of letters from would-be prospectors wanting to know which is the best, dry placering or wet placering.

There is a number of things to take into consideration when deciding whether to try your luck with one or the other.

Your background has a lot to do with it, also what time of the year you are going to go. There are times in the winter when you cannot drive to a lot of the placer grounds in the mountains and would not be able to stand the winter weather with some poor camping equipment and there is also parts of the summer when the average person cannot stand the heat of the desert and valleys in the dry placer districts.

If you are used to the cold weather and can stand the cold you can placer in the mountains all during the winter. Some of the boys I know about that are at an elevation of 5,000 feet, placer the year around. They have a cabin and lay in supplies for the winter, for their roads are usually blocked with snow. Usually the winter time is good placering for there is water available at places where you cannot get any water in the summer time. That is one of the best reasons for staying in the mountains in the winter time.

On the other hand, there are places on the desert and in the south where the heat becomes almost unbearable, but it is only at that time that the dirt becomes dry enough so that you can use dry placer equipment.

There is a place down in the Chocolate Mountains in California where it becomes really hot. So hot you dare not touch a piece of metal that has been lying in the sun. There is some arroyos there that have from three to four feet of overburden and the only way you can work those arroyos, that have some heavy concentrations under that overburden is to do so during that hot weather. You can uncover a stretch of ground one day and come back in a couple days and work the ground that has dried, by arranging your work at different places you can keep busy. You cannot work this ground before July 1st as it is a kind of ground that retains the moisture from the winter rains.

There are places in the desert though, where there is very little overburden in the arroyos and during the dry weather of the winter they can be worked. There is also some places where there is enough rain in the winter time to make it possible to use wet equipment at different times.

Most people like to be along the rivers where there is lots of water, where they can fish and hunt and placer at the same time. They only find these conditions in the mountains so they will have to take up the wet placering.

There are others that like that dry warm air of the desert. It is much healthier than the mountainous areas and if one is out for their health, the desert is the place to get used to, regardless of what kind of a climate you have been living in.

Half the battle of living in the desert is getting used to it. When you become accustomed to that heat you do not mind it much. I worked all one summer at a place where we went out at daylight, worked until about 8 a.m., rested during the day and went back to work at 5 p.m., and worked until dark. I enjoyed it and it was a very profitable summer.

Another thing—do you want to prospect and find some virgin ground that is rich? If you do, the desert is the place to go. You have much more chance of finding it there. That brings us back to that part of getting away from the highways. Believe me, there are places in the desert where you do get away from the highways, too. One place that I stumbled onto in the Arizona Desert was so interesting that I overlooked the fact that my grub was about gone, when I started to figure where would be the closest place to get supplies I found I was about equal distance from four different places in four different directions and not a one of them closer than seventy-five miles. That wouldn't have been far traveling in a car, but leading a packtrain of burros is a different proposition.

As the crow flies I wasn't possibly more than forty miles to one place, but the route I had to take would have made it twice that distance. I never did get back there and years afterward someone else found it and turned it into a paying proposition.

The Old Prospector is getting too old now to make trips to all those places he would like to revisit and use the modern equipment he has. But this younger generation that is taking up prospecting will go in those places with modern equipment and make some good strikes.

Up in Northern Nevada, not far from the Black Rock Desert, I prospected the hills all around one valley and found lots of leads but none of them good enough to work. In these trips I crossed and recrossed that valley and about ten years afterward, right down in that valley I had walked across a dozen times, they found some of the best placer ground in Nevada. I was a hard rock miner then and didn't pay any attention to placer gold.

The best way to decide on whether you want to dry placer or wet placer is to do a lot of reading before you start out, learn the experience of others. If you read books by authors that are written from experience and not from reference libraries, you will find a lot of knowledge that will tell you whether you will like the dry placering best or will want to stay up in the hills where the water runs and do your wet placering.

TWO GOOD BEGINNER BOOKS

GOLD IN PLACER — This book was written especially for the beginner prospector, the one that does not know anything about placer mining. It takes up each phase of the work and is written in a way that he can understand it. It takes him through all the work of a placer miner from the time the idea enters his head until the gold drops in the bottle and ready to sell to the buyer.

GOLD IN LODE — This book was also written for the beginner prospector. It tells him how to prospect for gold in lode in a systematic way and how to by-pass a lot of the troubles that average prospector has to contend with. It also has chapters on using different kinds of radio equipment and about the Geiger Counter and Mineralight.

Paper bound copies of the above two books will be mailed postpaid. Each $3.00.

If you are going to do any prospecting or mining you should obtain the Old Prospector's catalog. Prospectors supplies, mining books and anything that the prospector needs.

It will be mailed you free if you send your name and address.

Please mail all correspondence about this book or orders for books and blueprints and maps to

THE OLD PROSPECTOR

ol½ E. Edgeware Rd.   Los Angeles 26, Calif.

BLUEPRINTS OF MACHINES

Blueprint
Number   Machine

17   The Doodle Bug, a wet concentrator used in connection with a gasoline engine, pump and hose.

18   The Papoose (Rocking Sluice), a wet concentrator, handles fifty times as much dirt as a pan.

19   Hand Dry Washer. A dry concentrator for use where water is not available. Weight about 32 pounds.

20   Combination Grub Box & Table. Also drawing of how to make a home-made retort and concentrating bib.

21   Power Dry Washer. (Dry Concentrator). Weight about 50 pounds. Uses 2 cycle gas engine. Will keep one man busy shoveling.

22   Sluice Boxes. Blueprint shows different kinds, how set up and kind of screen and riffles to use.

163 Sampler Dry Washer. This is an 8 pound dry concentrator, can be folded and carried under your arm.

164 One Man Hoist. Made from old car chassis. Easy to build and for one man to operate, used in lode mining.

The above blueprints are all 15"x24" on heavy blueprint paper. Mailed postpaid for $1.00 each, or 3 for $2.00.